Christmas cards for you to make

1 Trace the snowman shape at the back of the book on to a piece of card.

2 Stick on cotton wool following the outline.

GLUE

3 Use cut out paper shapes for eyes, nose, mouth and buttons.

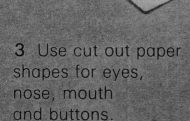

Add glitter for decoration.

Merry Christmas

Stick some Christmas ribbon on to a piece of card to look like...

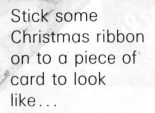

GLUE

...a wrapped parcel!

Write your message inside.

Fold a strip of card alternately backward and forward (it's called a Leporello fold) as many times as you like...

fold forward
fold back

CHRISTMAS GREETINGS

Paint a picture on the front.

Fold a piece of paper in half.

Then draw a tree shape. (You can use the pattern at the back of the book.)

Cut away half the tree...

...and decorate with snowflakes and stars.

MAKE A POP-UP CARD

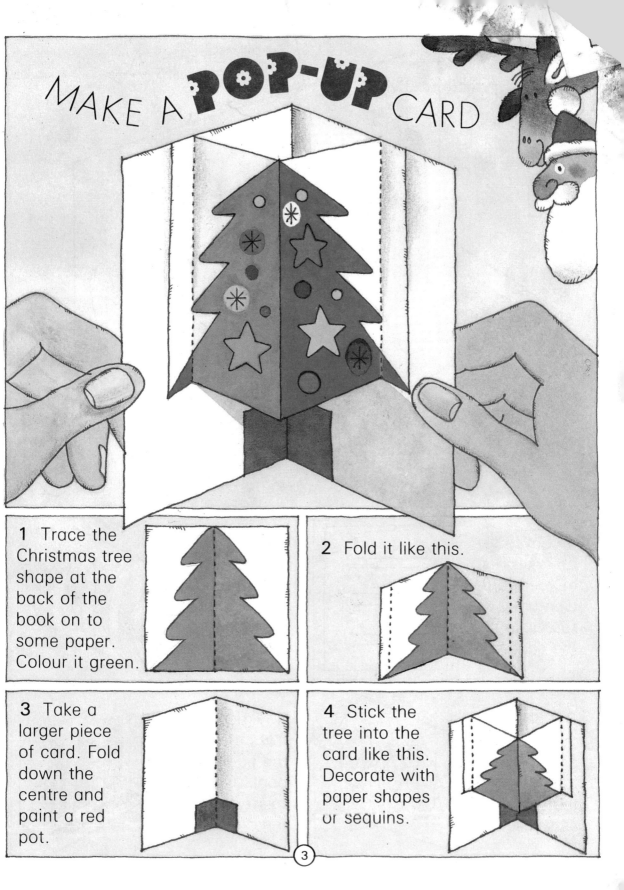

1 Trace the Christmas tree shape at the back of the book on to some paper. Colour it green.

2 Fold it like this.

3 Take a larger piece of card. Fold down the centre and paint a red pot.

4 Stick the tree into the card like this. Decorate with paper shapes or sequins.

③

The Three Kings POP-UP card

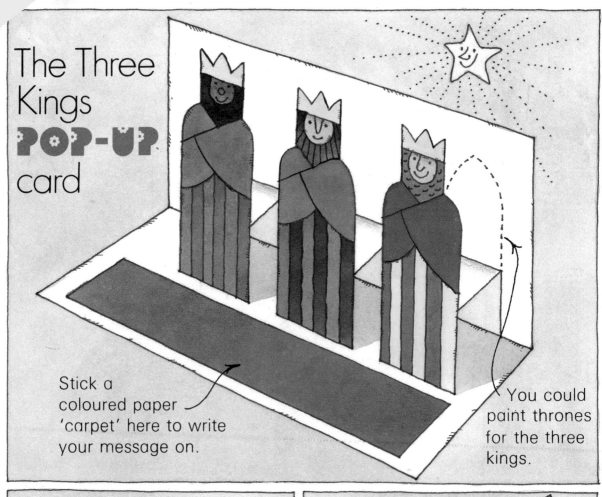

Stick a coloured paper 'carpet' here to write your message on.

You could paint thrones for the three kings.

1 Cut three pairs of slits in your card. Don't go too close to the edge.

cut

2 Fold the card in half, then thread a pencil through the slits to open them up.

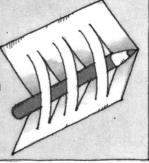

3 Take the pencil out and pinch the folds so that the card looks like this.

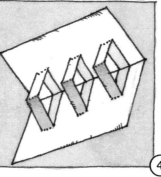

4 Trace three kings from the shape at the back of the book. Colour them and stick them in place.

Make a Christmas stocking

1 Cut out a stocking shape from newspaper. The top must be 20 cm across.

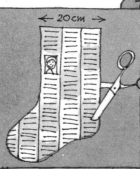

← 20 cm →

2 Pin the pattern to some felt. Cut out with pinking shears.

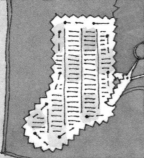

3 Glue or stitch round the edge of the stocking leaving the top open.

4 Add a loop of felt or ribbon to hang up the stocking.

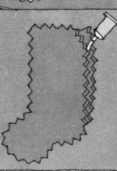

5 Add a felt top to the stocking and stick on Christmas shapes cut out of felt.

A SWEET TREE

1 Cut a good shaped branch and paint it any colour you like. Gold or silver would look pretty or you could wrap silver foil round the twigs.

2 Wedge the branch in a flower pot or box using a lump of Plasticine and tightly packed newspaper.

3 Put a layer of tissue paper on top of the newspaper. Stick cotton wool on some of the twigs to look like snow.

4 Tie loops of thread to some sweets and hang them on your 'tree'.

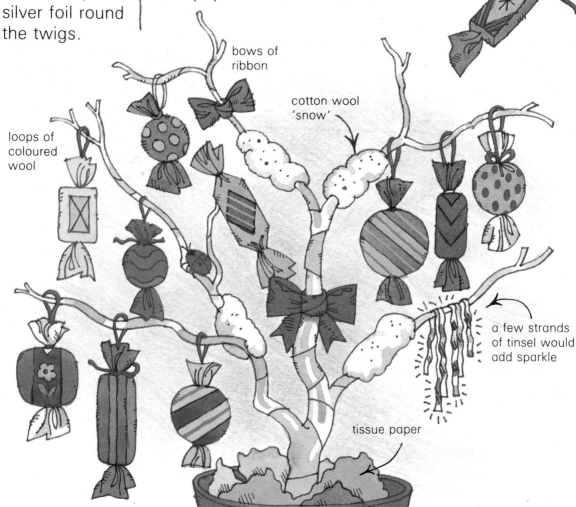

bows of ribbon

cotton wool 'snow'

loops of coloured wool

a few strands of tinsel would add sparkle

tissue paper

6

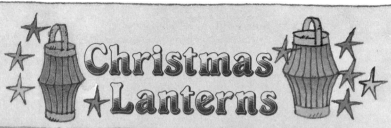

Christmas Lanterns

You could make lanterns from pretty wrapping paper or wallpaper...

...or make a garland by hanging lots of lanterns from a streamer.

You could hang your lantern on the Christmas tree.

1 Fold your paper in half lengthways. Draw a line 2 cm from the edge.

2 cm

2 Cut strips about 2 cm wide from the folded edge to the pencil line.

3 Open out the paper and glue along one of the short edges.

GLUE

4 Bend the paper round into a tube and stick the two short edges together.

5 Stick a loop of paper to the top of the lantern to make a handle.

stick here

SPECIAL SWEETS

No cooking!

You could wrap and hang these on your tree.
(see page 6)

You will need:
8 oz (227 g) icing sugar
1 small egg white
Flavouring (strawberry, banana or peppermint)
Food colouring*

1 Sieve the icing sugar into a bowl.

2 Whisk the egg white and add a few drops of flavouring and colouring **eg** strawberry and red colouring,* peppermint and green colouring.*

egg white

*If you prefer not to use food colouring, these sweets can be decorated by dipping half of each sweet into melted chocolate.

3 Add the egg white to the icing sugar and knead until the mixture is stiff and doughlike.

4 Roll into small balls

flatten the tops

and leave to harden.

Marzipan sweets

You will need:
A block of marzipan
Food colouring*
Raisins, nuts,
cherries etc
for decoration

1 Divide the marzipan into four pieces.

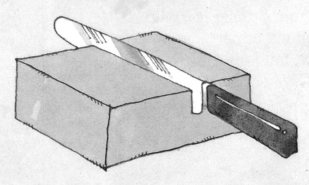

2 Add different food colouring to each piece and knead it in.

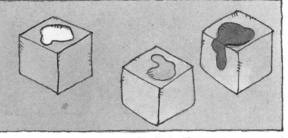

*The same sweets can be made without food colouring

3 Roll some of each colour marzipan into small balls and decorate with nuts, cherries, raisins, or 'hundreds and thousands'.

Sprinkle with icing sugar.

Or roll out four different coloured pieces into long sausages…

Push rolls into a square and flatten them on all sides.

Cut bite-size pieces and sprinkle with icing sugar.

Christmas crackers

1 Cover the cardboard tube from a toilet roll with crêpe paper. Leave enough at both ends to make a frill.

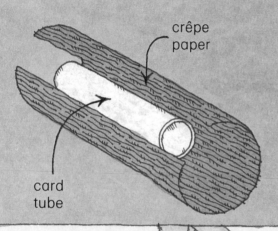

crêpe paper

card tube

2 Gather the crêpe paper at one end and fasten tightly with an elastic band.

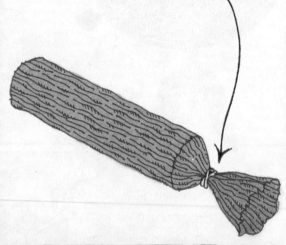

3 Drop sweets or small gifts into the tube and fasten this end.

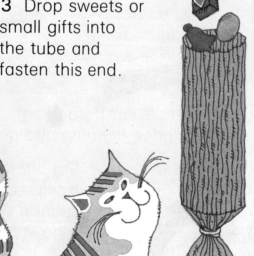

4 Decorate with stars, pieces of doily or pictures cut from old Christmas cards.

PAPER HATS

1 Use tissue paper or coloured paper.

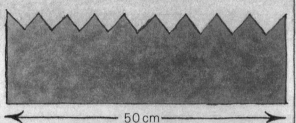

← 50 cm →

Cut out a shape like this 50 cm wide for a child or 60 cm wide for a grown up.

2 Join the two edges and stick firmly.

Then decorate with milk bottle tops, glitter, streamers or gummed shapes.

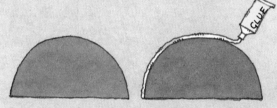

Or you can cut out two shapes like this.
Stick the curved edges together and decorate them to make a pirate's or a general's hat.

Or make a cone, stick streamers or feathers in the top and decorate as you like.

You can make paper hats to put in your crackers.

Make your own nativity scene

Set the scene on cardboard covered in straw or make a stable from a small cardboard box.

To make the people, first make a small ball from cotton wool or newspaper. Ask Mum for some clean old tights or stockings.

Push the ball into a piece of stocking, twist and tie.

To make the bodies, trace the shapes from the back of the book on to stiff paper or card.

Colour them blue for Mary, brown for Joseph, bright colours for kings and shepherds.

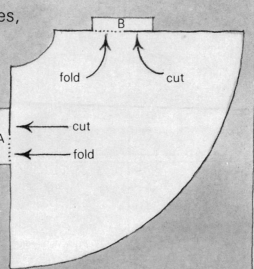

B

fold   cut

A

cut

fold

Bend tabs A and B outwards and slot them together.

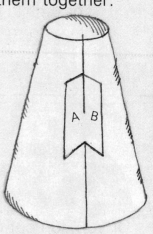

A B

Cut out arms from stiff paper and colour to match body.

You can cut off the tabs and just use sticky tape to join the cones if you prefer.

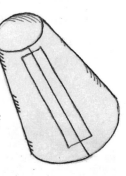

Next push the end
of the stocking head
into the body.

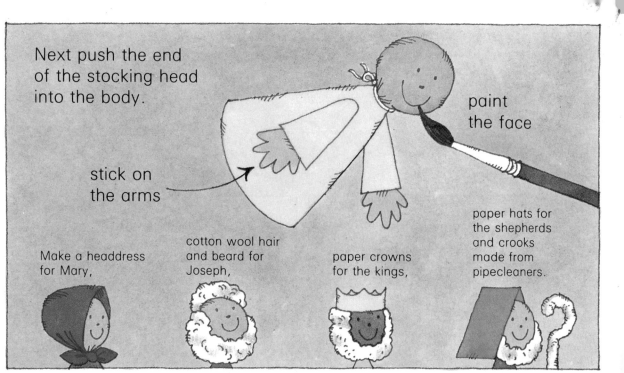

paint
the face

stick on
the arms

Make a headdress
for Mary,

cotton wool hair
and beard for
Joseph,

paper crowns
for the kings,

paper hats for
the shepherds
and crooks
made from
pipecleaners.

To make sheep,
stick four used
matches into one
side of a matchbox
to make legs.

Then cut out the
faces like this.
(see page 23)

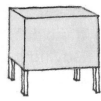

Stick the head on the box
and cover the body
with cotton wool.

(Use large matchboxes to
make cows!)

To make the manger, fold a
piece of paper like this.

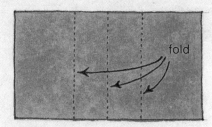

fold

Make a little Baby Jesus in the
same way that you made Mary
and place this in the manger.

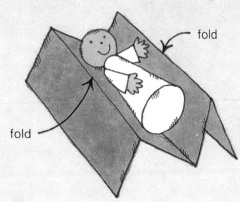

fold

fold

13

1 Stick old Christmas cards, paper plates or shapes cut out of card on to some ribbon.

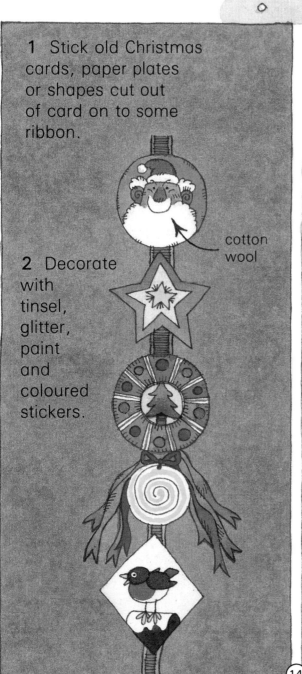

cotton wool

2 Decorate with tinsel, glitter, paint and coloured stickers.

1 Cut a circle of white paper and fold it in half three times.

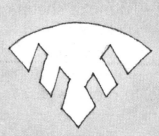

fold   fold   fold

2 Cut little pieces from the sides, leaving part uncut.

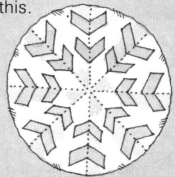

Open it out to look like this.

Hang your snowflakes on the Christmas tree or decorate your windows with them.

FRIEZES

1 Roll up a strip of crêpe paper loosely, then flatten it.

2 Cut out simple shapes to make your pattern.

3 Unroll your frieze and decorate with tinsel, glitter or thin paper strips.

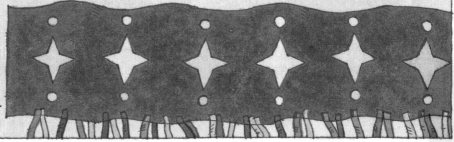

A Christmas tree frieze

Trace the tree shape from the back of the book on to a roll of crêpe paper.

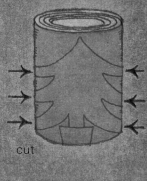

cut

Make sure some of the folded edge is uncut or it will fall to pieces!

Here it is opened out.

Silver bells

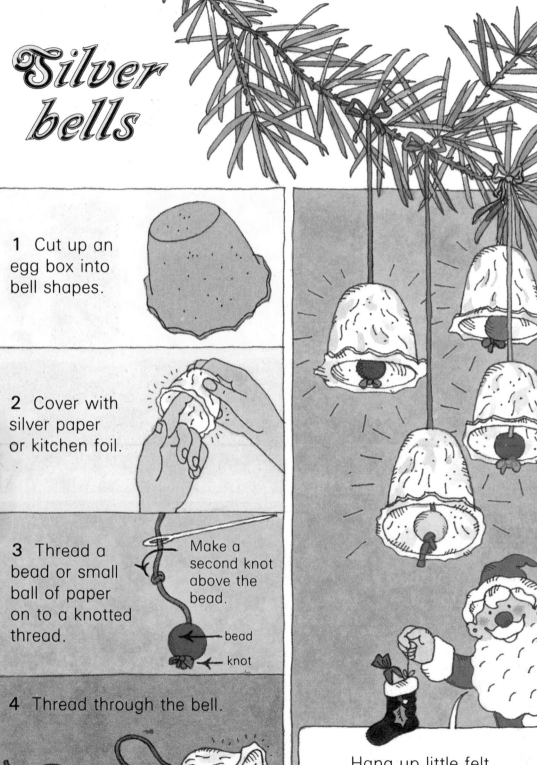

1 Cut up an egg box into bell shapes.

2 Cover with silver paper or kitchen foil.

3 Thread a bead or small ball of paper on to a knotted thread.

Make a second knot above the bead.

← bead
← knot

4 Thread through the bell.

Hang up little felt stockings with a sweet or small gift inside.

Fingerprint gift tags

Dip your fingers into ink or paint and make a print on a small piece of card. Draw in details of wings, feet, tails, ears and noses.

A TABLE DECORATION

The flame is made from a yellow piece of paper and a red piece.

Paint a toilet roll red or green.

Snip the bottom of the toilet roll, bend the tabs and stick here.

Paint a cheese spread box (or paper plate). Decorate with cotton wool, tinsel and glitter.

Add some ribbon and pine cones if you can find some.

Make an Advent calendar

During October and November collect twenty four empty matchboxes.

Cut a strip of card the same width as the long side of a matchbox. Stick the boxes to the card strip like this.

Glue a ribbon to the back of the card to hang up your calendar.

Decorate and number each box from 1 to 24.

Put a small present or sweet inside each box.

Open one drawer each day from 1st December.

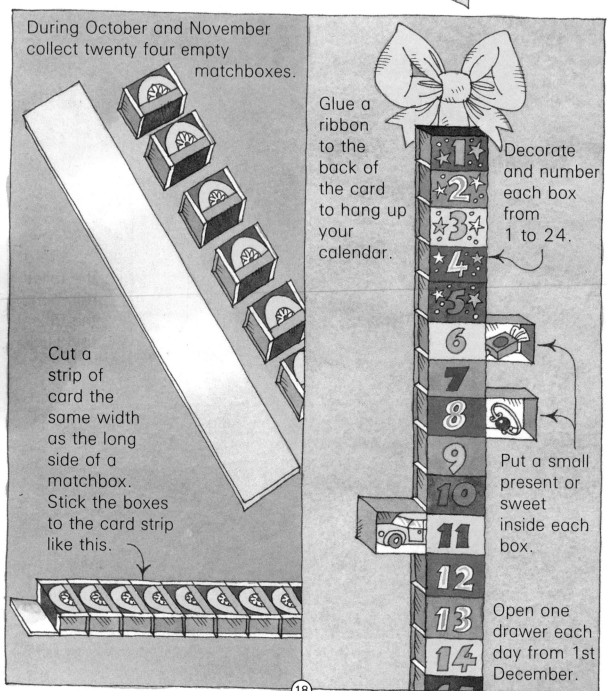

PAPER CHAINS

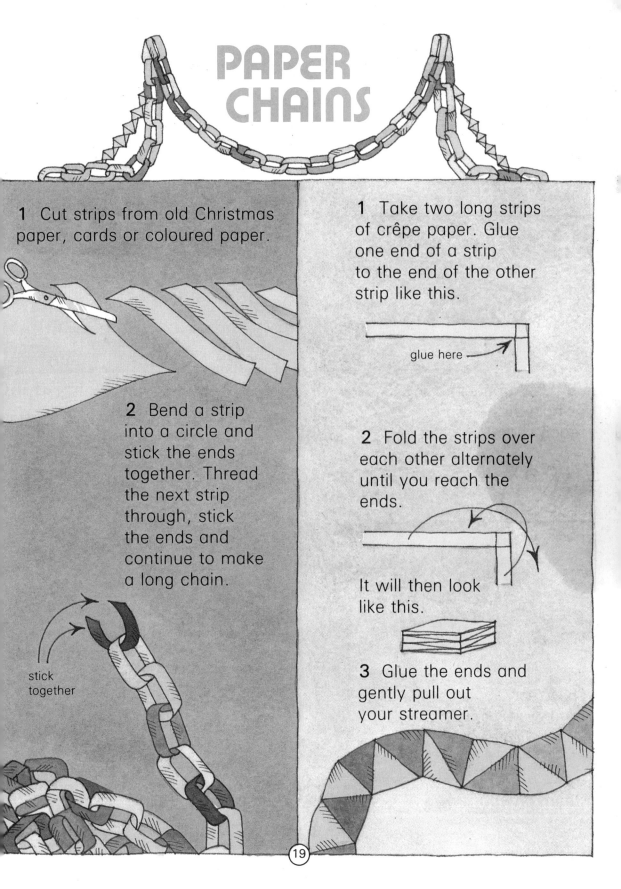

1 Cut strips from old Christmas paper, cards or coloured paper.

2 Bend a strip into a circle and stick the ends together. Thread the next strip through, stick the ends and continue to make a long chain.

stick together

1 Take two long strips of crêpe paper. Glue one end of a strip to the end of the other strip like this.

glue here

2 Fold the strips over each other alternately until you reach the ends.

It will then look like this.

3 Glue the ends and gently pull out your streamer.

Decorations made from clay

You will need:
2 cups plain flour
½ cup salt
Mix these with cold water and knead till smooth.

1 Roll out the clay.

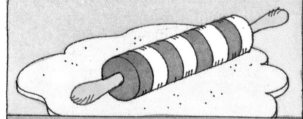

2 Use biscuit cutters or templates to make the shapes.

3 Use a pencil to poke a hole at the top of each shape.

4 Bake at 260°C (500°F, Gas 9) until they sound hollow when tapped.

5 When cool, paint and decorate with glitter. Thread cotton through the holes and hang them on your tree.

POTATO PRINT WRAPPING PAPER

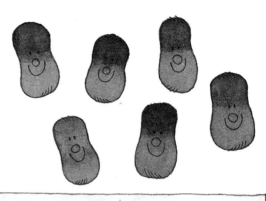

1 Cut a potato in half and draw a simple shape on it.

2 Cut away the potato round your shape so that it is raised.

3 Dip the potato in some paint. Press down on to a large sheet of paper and keep repeating this to make an all over pattern.

Shapes used in this book

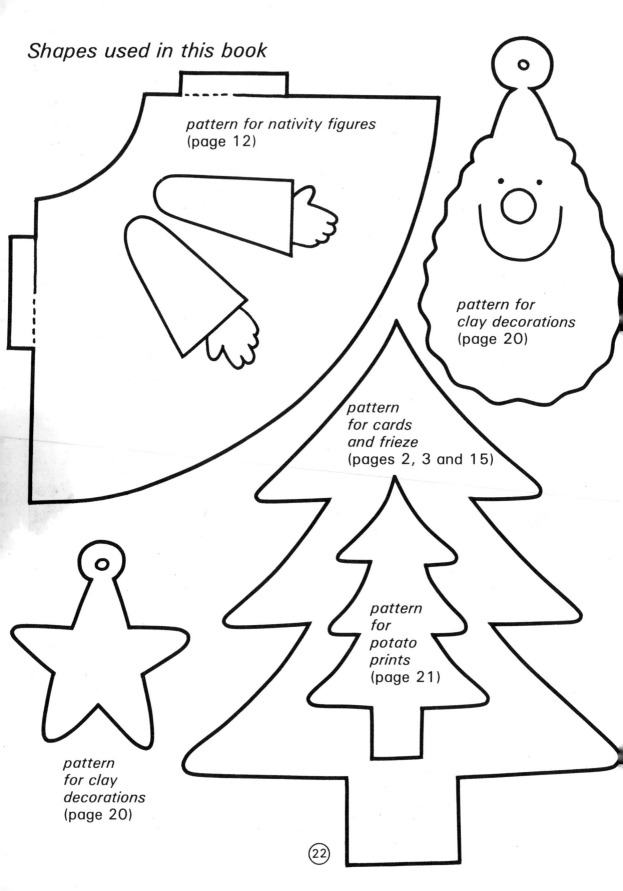

pattern for nativity figures
(page 12)

*pattern for
clay decorations
(page 20)*

*pattern
for cards
and frieze*
(pages 2, 3 and 15)

*pattern
for
potato
prints
(page 21)*

*pattern
for clay
decorations
(page 20)*

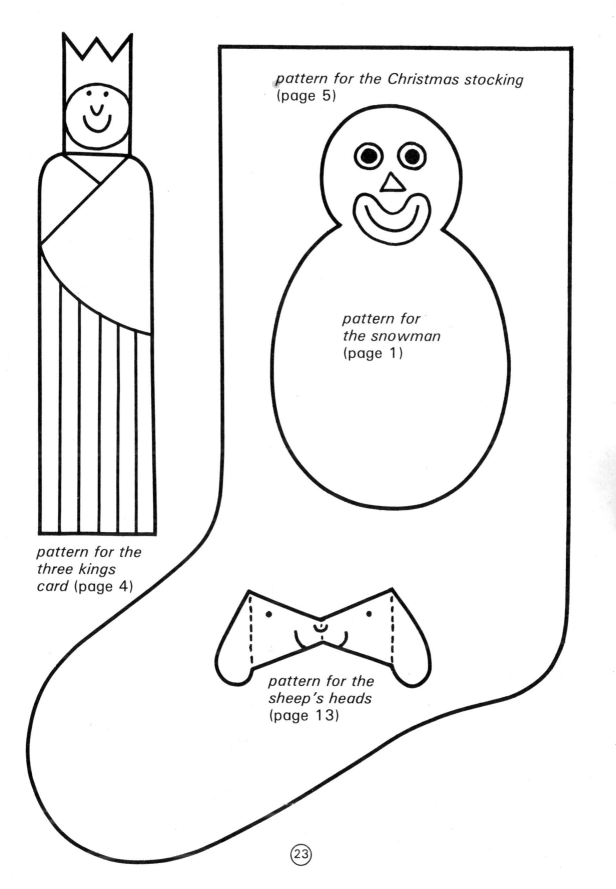

pattern for the Christmas stocking
(page 5)

pattern for
the snowman
(page 1)

pattern for the
three kings
card (page 4)

pattern for the
sheep's heads
(page 13)

23

Other useful Christmas shapes for cards and decorations